It's All Under Control Bible Study

A 6-Week
Guided Journey

It's All Under Control

Bible Study

Jennifer Dukes Lee

TYNDALE
MOMENTUM®

The nonfiction imprint of
Tyndale House Publishers, Inc.

Visit Tyndale online at www.tyndale.com.

Visit Tyndale Momentum online at www.tyndalemomentum.com.

Visit the author at jenniferdukeslee.com.

TYNDALE, Tyndale Momentum, and Tyndale's quill logo are registered trademarks of Tyndale House Publishers, Inc. The Tyndale Momentum logo is a trademark of Tyndale House Publishers, Inc. Tyndale Momentum is the nonfiction imprint of Tyndale House Publishers, Inc., Carol Stream, Illinois.

It's All Under Control Bible Study: A 6-Week Guided Journey

Designed by Eva M. Winters

The author is represented by the literary agency of Alive Literary Agency, 7680 Goddard St., Suite 200, Colorado Springs, CO 80920, www.aliveliterary.com.

For information about special discounts for bulk purchases, please contact Tyndale House Publishers at csresponse@tyndale.com, or call 1-800-323-9400.

ISBN 978-1-4964-3051-9

Printed in the United States of America

24   23   22   21   20
7   6   5   4

Contents

〰〰〰

Introduction *vii*
How to Get the Most Out of This Study *ix*

WEEK 1: Is Control Setting You Free or Making You Frazzled? *1*

WEEK 2: Intimacy with Jesus *19*

WEEK 3: Wild Obedience *41*

WEEK 4: Why You Need Help (and the Courage to Ask for It) *57*

WEEK 5: The Permission You Need to Rest *73*

WEEK 6: Under the Control of God Alone *85*

Epilogue *99*

Leader's Guide *101*
On Your Own Activities *105*
Endnotes *111*
About the Author *113*

Introduction

⋀⋀⋀⋀

EVERYONE DEALS with control issues. But almost no one wants to admit it—at least, not at first.

When I finally got honest about my own struggle with control, I heard so many women whisper the words: "You too?"

I always breathe a little easier when I know I'm not "the only one."

Guess what? You're not the only one either. You're not the only one who struggles with trusting God's plans for your life. You're not the only one who wants to maintain control in the midst of the chaos. You're not the only one who wants a well-marked map from Jesus but rarely gets one. You're not the only one who feels drained by the frenetic pace of trying to keep it "all under control."

There is great relief in realizing that you're not alone.

You are holding in your hands an invitation to leave behind your frazzled life to discover a peace you almost forgot was possible. I've created this practical, biblical guide so you can figure out what's yours to control and what's not. I pray that this will bring sanity and peace to your busy life.

So gather up some friends and prepare to meet some like-minded comrades in the pages of your Bible. Together we will take steps toward surrendering to the one who has it all under control: Jesus Christ.

I'm convinced that we will come out of this study trusting God more than ever before. With Scripture as our guide, we will let go of what God has *not* asked us to do so we can shine at what he *has*.

I'm ready for this.

You too?

Jennifer

How to Get the Most Out of This Study

∧∧∧∧

Along with this workbook, each person will need a pen or pencil and the following:

1. **A Bible.** I quote from the New International Version unless otherwise noted. If you don't have that version, you can find the text online on websites such as www.BibleGateway.com.

2. **My book *It's All Under Control*.** The book provides the framework for this study. Additionally, the book offers practical tips for "Cracking the Control Code." The suggested activities at the end of each chapter in *It's All Under Control*—as well as the diagrams and decision tools—help cement the key concepts of this Bible study while helping you apply them in your everyday life.

    At the beginning of each session, I've listed the chapters in my book that correlate to that material. As you read the related chapters, I encourage you to highlight anything that resonates with you. What seems surprising, challenging, or remarkably familiar to your own experience? Consider how it relates to that week's session.

3. **A commitment to complete each session.** This study will ask something of you beyond simply filling in the blanks. You are about to embark on a journey toward trusting God like never before. You will grow most if you:

    ▸ Ask God to reveal his heart to you as you respond to the questions and prompts.

    ▸ Get honest with God, yourself, and others about your fears, doubts, experiences, and patterns of behavior.

    ▸ Put into practice what Scripture asks of you. As Jesus' own brother James told us, we are called to do more than read our Bibles: "Do what it says. Anyone who listens to the word but does not do what it says is like someone who looks at his face in a mirror and, after looking at himself, goes away and immediately forgets what he looks like" (James 1:22-24).

    I know you are a busy woman. This study was designed especially for women like you. Here's a confession: At times in my life, it's been hard for me to invest time to dig in and study God's Word. I have worried that if I spent time with God, I'd miss something else I was supposed to be doing. But here's the life-changing truth of the matter: You will never regret time spent with Jesus. And you will never regret a decision to trust God.

HERE'S WHAT YOU'LL FIND IN EACH WEEK'S STUDY

A key Bible verse: Each passage will relate to that week's content. I encourage you to memorize these verses.

My Story: I'll go first by sharing a bit of my struggle.

Your Story: You'll have an opportunity to get honest about your feelings, doubts, fears, and attitudes before you dig into the Scriptures.

Their Story: The Bible is filled with stories from people who struggled like you and I do. Each week, you'll learn and grow from their stories.

Getting Your Control Under Control: This is an opportunity to reflect on the week's lessons and apply them to your everyday life.

Prayer: There's no better way to end each lesson than by asking God to sink his truths deep into your heart and give you the strength to trust and obey him. Whether you pray in a group or on your own, committing yourself to God has genuine power to transform your life.

You'll also have the opportunity to go deeper with **On Your Own** activities, if you choose.

ESPECIALLY FOR LEADERS

I am so glad you said yes to Jesus by leading this study. You, my friend, have been equipped for this. At the same time, I know you are busy, so I have put together a leader's guide full of tips, ideas, and resources to take the guesswork out of heading a group. See page 101 for a full guide.

Is Control Setting You Free or Making You Frazzled?

∧∧∧∧

I am not the Christ.

JOHN 1:20

∧∧∧∧

WEEK 1 FOCUS

▸ To identify how pervasive the problem of control truly is

▸ To get a sense of what it looks like to trust God more fully

LET'S GET STARTED

Read the introduction and chapters 1, 2, and 3 of *It's All Under Control.*

For a bonus teaching video from Jennifer based on this week's session, visit www.ItsAllUnderControlBook.com/Resources.

Why did you say yes to this study? What do you hope to gain by the end of our journey together?

MY STORY

I read once that surrender is what happens when God hands you a blank piece of paper with a space for you to sign your name at the bottom and then you hand it back to him to fill in as he wills. For a woman who wants to have it "all under control," that kind of surrender terrifies me!

When I began this journey with Jesus, I asked myself: What would it look like to have blank-paper trust with God? What would it look like to open my fists in order to receive God's best for my life?

That's our goal for the next six weeks. My hope is that when we get to the last page of this study, we will trust God like never before. Together we are going to figure out what to hang on to and what to let go of. We are going to figure out what's ours to control and what isn't.

So much of life feels out of control, doesn't it? Every morning, Twitter tells us about another terror attack, a mass shooting, a hurricane, a wildfire. It seems as if Earth is one big emergency.

Even if we're not in the middle of a crisis, everyday life feels chaotic. We do our best to wrap our hands around everything: our busy schedules, our children, our work responsibilities, our relationships. We want to have it "all under control," but most of the time, life feels anything but.

In the first chapter of my book (see pages 8–9), I write honestly about my own struggle with control:

Confession: I have loved the steady comfort of control—even though it was only an illusion.

Control had become a coping mechanism to numb myself from the pain of life. I believed that even if I couldn't control the big things, I could at least *try* to control the little stuff: what I put in my mouth, how many steps I tallied on my Fitbit, my gray hairs, how I scheduled every minute of every day, what you thought about me when I talked with you. . . .

I've generally been able to handle a lot of tasks at once, and I've always been an achiever who won't easily back down from a challenge. Hard work has never scared me. But I can't begin to tell you how much my inner achiever propels me into dangerously high gear. . . .

All of this doing and striving was supposed to bring me happiness. With great surprise, I realized that it wasn't working out that way at all. Trying to wrap my arms around everything and everyone felt like attempting to herd baby kittens.

YOUR STORY
Describe the last time your attempts to manage something in your life felt like an exercise in herding baby kittens.

How pervasive is the issue of control? Do you think it's something everyone deals with? Or are some people "cured" of the desire to control?

We can probably all think of women in our lives who seem to be free-spirited, employing a *whatever happens, happens* philosophy. Let's call them the Free Spirits. We can probably also think of women who feel responsible for many things, do a lot of those things really well, but can end up feeling frazzled and weary under all that pressure. Let's call them Frazzled Spirits.

On the continuum below, where would you put yourself? Mark an X on the spot.

←- →

FREE SPIRIT   FRAZZLED SPIRIT

When was the last time you felt frazzled on account of all you believed you needed to do, oversee, or manage?

The more frazzled and out of control my life gets, the more I try to control it. That sometimes results in even more frazzle! It's a vicious cycle. Is that your experience too? Why or why not?

Here's a list of areas that women often feel the need to control. Which ones strike you personally? Circle those. Try not to overthink your answers.

My weight

Job responsibilities

My thoughts

My children

The future

The past

My health

My house

Anger

Finances

Wrinkles

What I eat

My attitude

My husband/boyfriend

My friends

My to-do list

What people think of me

Current projects

Decisions affecting my extended
   family

Safety concerns with kids

A difficult relationship

My schedule

My perspective

The quality of my work

Other: _____

Control. When we hear that word, we often bristle. Our minds tend to drift toward negative connotations of the word. For example: *She's such a control freak. He's such a controlling narcissist. Why is she so hyper about every little detail?*

But not all areas leave us frazzled—and we shouldn't jump to the conclusion that *all* control is bad. Notice that some of the items in the list on page 5 carry a more positive connotation, and in fact, God calls us to live a life of self-control. Furthermore, most people agree that if we gain control of our attitude and perspective, we will be healthier, calmer people. So in those cases, we aren't frazzled, we're free, which reveals that some control is actually a good thing! For instance, some control over your children or your workplace might be in order. Good management often leads to a sense of calm and well-being.

The danger comes when we find ourselves slipping from healthy control to unhealthy control, from free to frazzled.

Here are a few examples to demonstrate the difference between the two.

Weight

- ▸ *Healthy control is:* following your doctor's orders to manage your weight.
- ▸ *Unhealthy control is:* excessively counting calories and following strict, self-imposed food rules with detrimental results such as eating disorders.

Finances

- ▸ *Healthy control is:* being a good steward of your finances.
- ▸ *Unhealthy control is:* monitoring and questioning every purchase your spouse makes.

To-Do Lists

- ▸ *Healthy control is:* saying yes to a God-given assignment and adding it to the list.
- ▸ *Unhealthy control is:* feeling like you need to say yes to every opportunity and every request, resulting in an overburdened life and an overwhelming list.

Family

- *Healthy control is:* offering to host your family's Thanksgiving dinner when your aging grandmother no longer can do so.
- *Unhealthy control is:* telling every member exactly what to bring to Thanksgiving dinner—along with the recipes they are to follow.

With these comparisons in mind, review the list on page 5 once more. Put an X beside any area where you sometimes slip into unhealthy control.

Friend, it takes a lot of guts to admit our struggle with unhealthy control. Congratulations on risking vulnerability. We can't fix what we're not willing to admit is broken. I'm right here with you, with my own hand raised.

Now, as best as you're able, describe in a couple of sentences what might cause you to fall into areas of unhealthy control. Is there something you fear will happen if you don't take control?

We become frazzled not only when we're trying hard to manage too much, but when our efforts are driven by anxiety. I don't know about you, but when I get fearful, I make a plan! I believe my plans will ensure security for my children, assuage my fears about the future, and keep everyone headed in the right general direction. Do I sound a little type A here? Are you that way too? Tell me I'm not alone.

Heaven knows that we want type-A planners in charge of sewage-treatment plants, operating rooms, airplane flight patterns, and the catered meals at our weddings.

But as my friend Cheri once told me, our plans and type-A behaviors can get out of hand. Cheri's father worked in the medical field, where a mistake could result in death. At one point in her life, Cheri said, "I took that same level of control to karaoke, to charades—to anything that involved spontaneity—because I didn't know the difference." As it turns out, she noted, incorrectly recording someone's lab results and singing the wrong notes in karaoke are two very different things.

Friend, God calls us to use our skills to make the world a better place. He calls us to be wise planners with our time and resources. Our ability to think ahead and predict possible outcomes is part of what distinguishes us from animals. Yet God asks us to hold our plans loosely, recognizing that our understanding of the future is limited while his is limitless. I'll bet you know the old saying "If you want to make God laugh, tell him your plans."

I'll bet you know an even older saying from Solomon's book of wise sayings. Read and reflect on Proverbs 16:9. Fill in the blanks. "In their hearts humans _____ their course, but the LORD _____ their steps."

THEIR STORY

Let's take a moment to look back on our collective history as the people of God. The human desire to control and plan is as old as time. In fact, control is a thematic thread that runs straight through the Bible—from beginning to end.

- ► At the start of the biblical narrative, Adam and Eve ate fruit from a forbidden tree (Genesis 3:6). Ultimately, they wanted control in the form of wisdom.
- ► In the middle of the narrative, religious leaders wanted to control the people. Because Jesus was a threat to that control, they plotted to kill him (Mark 3:6).

▶ In the end, the book of Revelation is ultimately about who will control the world.

There are hundreds of control moments in between. Throughout the Bible, we encounter numerous people who had a plan and wanted to wield a bit of control over a situation. Some of those people had a healthy relationship with control, but others didn't.

Let's meet a few of them.

Healthy control

Turn to Genesis 6:9-22 for an example of healthy control. As you read the passage, note each time a well-detailed plan and a bit of healthy control was beneficial. What most impresses you about the task set before Noah?

The Bible doesn't say exactly how long it took Noah to build that ark, but scholars agree that it would have taken decades. Imagine the planning required to build a boat the length of one and a half football fields and as high as a four-story building. The Bible doesn't say specifically, but it's certainly plausible that people mocked Noah. If so, imagine the self-control required to keep moving forward despite opposition. Imagine the plans needed to gather "every kind of food" (Genesis 6:21) to feed all those animals, as well as Noah's family. And think of the organizational skill required to gather up all those lumbering, skittering, slithering, flying, and sprinting animals. Scholars have estimated that about 45,000 animals would have fit into Noah's ark.

Read Genesis 7:4 to find out how long it took Noah to make final preparations and get every animal and his family settled into the ark. Write the length of time here: _____

That's not much time, people. If it were me, I would have left the snakes and spiders behind—and then blamed the tight deadline. But Noah, a man of obedience, did what he was told.

Where did he get his plan? Read Genesis 6:22 to find out. Fill in the blank. "Noah did everything just as _____ commanded him."

Noah was a man with a plan—a plan that was set in his hands by God. Noah also had the stamina to follow through on a long-term commitment. There are a lot of reasons why his obedience, his perseverance, and his healthy control make quite a difference to each of us today. Here's one big reason.

Turn to Luke 3:23-38, and skim over the list. This is one branch of the family tree of Jesus. Who is one of Jesus' ancestors? See if you find the familiar name of a shipbuilder in verse 36:

Noah teaches us that when we are in a state of healthy control, we can be used by God to accomplish his plans in this world. Those God-given assignments might have ripple effects that outlive us—and change the world for good.

Unhealthy control

Now let's take a look to see where trying to take control didn't end well—what we're calling unhealthy control.

Remember the Israelites? God made a promise to them while they were still in slavery.

Read the following passage and underline the verbs that reveal God's promises to them.

> I am the LORD, and I will bring you out from under the yoke of the Egyptians. I will free you from being slaves to them, and I will redeem you with an outstretched arm and with mighty acts of judgment. I will take you as my own people, and I will be your God.
>
> EXODUS 6:6-7

God followed through on his plans and his promises. He freed the Israelites (Exodus 12:31), miraculously parted a sea (Exodus 14:22), gave them food (Exodus 16:4), and provided water (Exodus 17:6). Though the Lord divinely and repeatedly provided for the Israelites, they often grumbled and wavered. At one point, they actually said they would have preferred to die in slavery back in Egypt (Exodus 16:3)!

The Israelites were gripped by fear, despite the fact that God had come through for them in mind-blowing ways. In the Scriptures, you can note how quickly they forgot God's provisions and how they assumed their own plans were better than his.

Read Exodus 15:22-24. How many days after that miraculous march through the parted Red Sea did it take before the Israelites started grumbling? _____

Only three days. My, my, we are an impatient, forgetful people. We're fooling ourselves if we say we wouldn't do the same thing as the Israelites! In his goodness, God sweetened the water (Exodus 15:25). Then when their bellies started grumbling, God sent a miracle food from heaven called manna.

Read Exodus 16:19. What were the instructions about storing this heaven-sent food?

Like us, the Israelites felt the urge to make their own plans, just in case God didn't come through.

What did the Israelites decide to do instead? How did that turn out for them? Read Exodus 16:20 and record your answer.

(And all the people said, "Ewwwww.")

Fast-forward to today. God promises throughout Scripture that he's got us covered. We say we trust God. We might even have the right Bible verses underlined and everything! But still our actions betray our fears. We try to take matters into our own hands, and in this modern age, it's easier than ever to trick ourselves into thinking we can do it on our own.

We've become so scarily self-sufficient—even as Christians. We believe in God, but we don't actually rely on him. We manage our lives instead of living them. We pray, "Give us this day our daily bread," but if we run out of bread, we drive the Escalade to Costco to buy in bulk what we don't really need anyway. (*It's All Under Control*, page 36)

If we've got it all under control, why are we so wrecked and weary?

So often our actions reveal that we trust our own plans more than God's. If we *do* surrender something to God, we are tempted to check back on his progress. (Tell me I'm not the only one to "help" God when he didn't actually ask for it.)

In short, we can act like self-appointed saviors to fix the people and problems in our lives. That is why it pays to listen for God's direction. Noah and the Israelites are proof that sometimes God calls us to *stand up* (as Noah did); at other times, he calls us to *stand by* (as the Israelites often failed to do).

Stand up

Like Noah, you may be asked to fulfill an assignment that requires great bravery. Stand up! Be fully you, with all your gifts and talents and ambition.

What does Hebrews 11:7 tell us about what compelled Noah to build the ark? Where do you sense God calling you to stand up and be brave? Or where have you sensed this in the past?

Stand by

Other times, like the Israelites, you will be asked to stand by. God is working out his plans in places you can't yet see.

According to Exodus 14:13-14, what did God ask the Israelites to do when the Egyptian army chased them soon after their escape? Where do you sense God calling you to stand by and wait? Or where have you sensed this in the past?

GETTING YOUR CONTROL UNDER CONTROL

John the Baptist shows us what it looks like to let God be God. When he first began preaching out in the wilderness, all kinds of people were asking who the goofy-dressed guy was. John let everyone know who he *was* by first telling everyone who he *wasn't*.

Let's see how the Bible describes John—and how John describes himself. Read the following verses and fill in the blanks.

There was a man sent from God whose name was John. . . . He himself was _____ the light; he came only as a witness to the light. (John 1:6, 8)

They asked him, . . . "Are you Elijah?" He said, "I am _____." (John 1:21)

"Among you stands one you do not know. He is the one who comes after me, the straps of whose sandals I am _____ worthy to untie." (John 1:26-27)

What's the common word that you inserted in the blank spaces above?
_____

Now for the kicker. Who else did John say he was not?

"I am not the _____." (John 1:20)

On Your Own

A great way to apply these biblical principles to your everyday life is by completing the "Cracking the Control Code" exercises introduced in *It's All Under Control.*

The control code is what I call the system of ideas, rules, and behaviors that we have set for ourselves to keep our lives in order. We want to crack that code so we can understand why we operate the way we do. Then we can replace those old systems with healthy living.

In this week's exercises, you'll create an inventory of what weighs you down in your life ("Running Smarter," page 105); identify times in your life when good intentions went south ("I Am Not the Christ," page 106); and pinpoint what gives you your identity ("Who Are You?," page 107). You can also download these resources at www.ItsAllUnderControlBook.com/Resources.

Let's call it the Great Ministry of *Not*.

When it comes down to it, we sometimes function like we are gods of our own lives. But we are *not*. I like how the 1984 edition of the New International Version renders John the Baptist's words in John 1:20: "I am not the Christ." (The terms *Messiah* and *Christ* both mean "the anointed one.")

Repeat after John the Baptist: "I am not the Christ." We know this truth in theory, but when we try to take control of what was never ours to control, we are playing God.

Ultimately, we've got to settle this issue of identity. We have reaffirmed, above, who we *aren't*. So then that raises the question: *Who are we?*

Read 1 John 3:1. Record who God says you truly are below.

No one ever asked you to be God. Instead, the truth is, you *belong* to God. You are a daughter. And because you belong to him, he will call on you to partner with him in some pretty amazing stuff. He will call you to do great things with the right amount of healthy control. And he will call on you to let go of areas where you are experiencing unhealthy control. He wants you to live as a free, not a frazzled, daughter of the King!

PRAYER

Let's pray that, over the next several weeks, God will reveal what's ours to control and what's not. Consult your list on page 5 and fill in the lines of the prayer on the next page with areas where you are currently in danger of crossing into unhealthy control.

Dear Lord, I know your ways are perfect and your plans are far better than my own. Make me brave to stand up *and take hold of what you've put within my reach. And compel me to* stand by *when you actually want me to wait while you work. Today, I confess the areas where I am tempted to take control of people and situations that I need to fully surrender to you:*

_____

_____

_____

_____

_____

_____

I am not the Christ. But I am loved deeply by the Christ. Help me to live as one beloved. In Jesus' name, amen.

Intimacy with Jesus

ᐯᐯᐯᐯ

*Though you have not seen him, you love him; and even though
you do not see him now, you believe in him and are filled
with an inexpressible and glorious joy.*

1 PETER 1:8

ᐯᐯᐯᐯ

WEEK 2 FOCUS

▸ To begin to understand how our lack of trust hinders intimacy with Jesus

▸ To uncover how trust issues keep us from surrendering control to God

LET'S GET STARTED

Read chapters 4, 5, and 6 of *It's All Under Control.*

For a bonus teaching video from Jennifer based on this week's session, visit www.ItsAllUnderControlBook.com/Resources.

LAST WEEK, we ended our time together with a prayer, asking God to reveal what's ours to control and what's not. We asked God to help us surrender areas where we have entered into a state of unhealthy control.

How has this awareness of unhealthy control affected you in the past week? Have you noticed changes in your thinking and reactions? Are there areas where you've been able to "let go" a little more? Are there areas where that's been especially difficult?

It can be challenging to know what's ours to control and what's not because emotions and feelings can get in the way. We feel as if it's our responsibility to help, to get involved, and to manage outcomes. *If I don't do it,* we ask ourselves, *who will? If I don't take charge,* we tell ourselves, *people I love might get hurt.* But what if there was a way to cut through all that emotion and fear to arrive at a place of discernment? There is a way.

This week, we'll focus on nurturing the single-most important relationship of our lives: our relationship with the Lord. This relationship is the only one that can cut through our complicated emotions, so we can:

- ▸ know when to hang on and when to let go
- ▸ make trusting God a habit
- ▸ arrive at decisions based on truth instead of emotion

MY STORY

A beautiful woman sat across the table from me every week at Bible study. Often I stole glances at her over the top of my workbook as she tilted her head and flipped through the Scriptures. She could find Ezra as easily as Genesis. Plus she had great hair. And a gorgeous smile. I was tempted to be a little jealous.

The Bible says Moses came down from the mountain with a shiny face because he had been in the presence of God. Call me crazy, but I think that sort of thing can still happen in the twenty-first century. If you took one look at this woman, you'd believe it too. You can't buy *that* look from Rodan + Fields. This woman wore her love for Scripture on her face, and let me tell you: She lit up the room when she started talking about the Lord.

One night at Bible study, someone read a passage from 1 Peter. After the passage was read, she put her hands flat down on her Bible and gasped out loud as if this were the first time she'd ever read such a beautiful thing in all her ever-lovin' life. Even though—*and I'm not exaggerating*—it was probably the 651st time she had read it.

Just so you know, she's been at this Bible-reading thing awhile. Did I mention that this woman is in her nineties? Meet Almarie. She is a wonder and a picture of what it means to have a deeply meaningful, heart-changing personal relationship with Jesus—the kind that radiates in a room.

Almarie's countenance changed, though, when we began discussing a certain passage that tells us that, without deeds, our faith is dead (see James 2:17). The sparkle in her eyes faded, and the corners of her mouth drooped a bit. What, she asked us, could a ninetysomething lady living in an assisted-living complex practically *do*?

We could tell Almarie felt frustrated, so we reached across the table with our words and our hands to assure her: *You have lived, and continue to live, a life of purpose—right where you are.*

It's easy for any of us to believe otherwise, isn't it?

Isn't there an Almarie in each of us? We're looking across tables, even at Bible studies, comparing notes and assuming that everyone else has got it all figured out. Culture is hawking the idea that you must make a name for yourself, climb higher, add another line to the résumé.

We get things twisted up, thinking that's what God wants of us, too. Like he's tallying up our "success" on a dry-erase board in the throne room. But scorecards can't measure our relationship with Jesus. Our relationship with him isn't built on the volume of our good deeds or by how busy we've been for the Kingdom.

No. Our relationship is built on trust.

Sometimes the hardest thing we can do is to stop *doing* so much. After all, our culture encourages us to consistently look as if we have everything together. It also places great value on our busyness, as if worth lies somewhere between the lines of our calendar boxes.

Almarie knew the truth about what really matters. Believe me: She's *lived* that. But that night at Bible study, she needed a few girlfriends to remind her. (Don't we all?)

A few minutes later, Almarie told us about what happens at 3:30 a.m. Every. Single. Night. The sparkle returned to her eyes as she spoke: "The Lord wakes me up. When I go to bed, I am so happy because I know he's going to wake me up at 3:30."

She gets out of bed, picks up her Bible, walks to her easy chair, and starts reading where she left off the night before. She reads and prays—for *a whole hour.*

"I know when I'm done, after about an hour, because I feel such a peace come over me." She shook her head, like she didn't quite know how else to describe such a holy encounter. "And then I go right back to bed, and I don't wake up 'til morning."

Intentional. Beautiful. Holy. This is a relationship of trust. This is what it means to have intimacy with our Lord.

But can I confess something to you? That level of intimacy sort of scares me—and not just because I want to sleep at 3:30 in the morning.

I go overboard in planning so much of my life because it seems less scary than the alternative. The alternative is intimacy with God. The closer I get to God, the greater the chance that I'm going to recognize his voice. And when I recognize his voice, there's a greater possibility that I'm going to hear him speaking into my heart, and I might not like what he tells me. (*It's All Under Control*, page 104)

The short version is this: I want to live my life for him, but at times, I've been scared of getting to truly know the one who created that life for me.

YOUR STORY

What's getting in your way of deeper intimacy with and trust in God?

To begin moving toward greater trust in God, take a few moments to consider your current level of trust in him.

On the line below, mark the place that best reflects your trust in God.

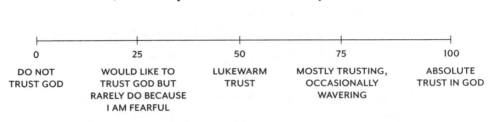

Friend, thank you for your honesty. Maybe you are like Almarie, with absolute trust. We are so grateful for women like you, who show us what it means to stand firm with unwavering faith, even as the winds of change blow. Or perhaps you are like many of us who waver from time to time. God wants to strengthen each of us and help us put down strong roots, so that when the winds blow, we will be found standing.

Why did you pick that spot on the line above? What do you think influences your level of trust in God?

Whether you're a church leader, a lifelong believer, someone who just met Jesus the day before yesterday, or someone who has strayed far from the faith, Jesus is wooing you to a place of deeper trust in him.

A multitude of factors keep us from trusting God. Here are five major obstacles:

Lack of silence and stillness. We get so busy that we can't hear the voice of God. As a result, we are unable to build a relationship with him.

Fear of the future. We believe that God will let us down if we give him control.

Past betrayal. Trust has been broken with authority figures or close loved ones in the past, shaping our present-day view of God.

Control. We desire to do things our own way.

Disappointment. We've trusted God in the past but feel that he let us down or didn't come through.

Which of those five obstacles ring truest to you? Circle one (or more). Feel free to add any additional reasons below.

We'll spend our entire lesson this week on trusting God, because it's the key to letting go of the things he never intended for us to control. Here are two key truths to remember as we go through this week's study:

1. You cannot trust someone you don't know.
2. You will never know whether you can trust Jesus if you don't give him the chance to prove himself trustworthy.

In short, trust requires two *R*s: relationship and risk.

Let's spend a little time exploring that first *R*, relationship. Think about the current or past relationships you've had with other people. I suspect that we all have people whom we have come to trust more than others. Think of the person you have trusted most in your life. **Write his or her name or initials here:** _____

What led you to feel a sense of trust toward this person?

I would imagine that your trust in this person came as a result of real and rich relationship, built over time. That was certainly true for me as I grew closer to my husband before our marriage.

> The more time I spent with Scott, the more I loved him. The more I loved him, the more I wanted to know everything about him: his interests, his habits, and his favorite food, rock band, color, song, books, jokes, cities, movies, restaurants, sports, and more. I couldn't get enough.
>
> The more I came to know Scott, the more I came to trust him.
> (*It's All Under Control*, page 107)

Trusting people requires relationship, built over time. It also requires the other *R*, risk. You have to open your heart to them.

Trust with God is built in the same way. You have to invest time with him—through prayer, Scripture reading, and worship—to build the relationship. And then you have to risk by letting go. You won't know if you can trust Jesus until you give him the chance to prove himself trustworthy.

In what ways have you seen relationship and risk being foundationally tied to your trust in God and/or people?

What areas of your life have you tried hard to control because you lack trust in people or in God?

THEIR STORY

We know from experience that even those we've deemed trustworthy can break our trust. We also know that our spiritual ancestors felt the same disappointment and sadness when people they had come to love and trust betrayed them.

Take, for instance, King David. He was a man of great power and influence. Scriptural evidence suggests that the king surrounded himself with people whom he believed to be trustworthy leaders. One of those people was a friend named Ahithophel. In fact, David had so much faith in Ahithophel that he made him one of his advisers.

Turn to 2 Samuel 15:12. Below, write down the descriptive noun that suggests the relationship with Ahithophel was built on trust.

During this time, David's son Absalom conspired to create a national rebellion against David. What did David's counselor Ahithophel do once the revolt began? Read 2 Samuel 15:31 and fill in the blanks.

Now David had been told, "Ahithophel is among the _____

_____."

A friend turned into a foe. A counselor into a conspirator. An adviser into an adversary.

Imagine David's heartbreak. In fact, you don't have to imagine it. You can read about it.

Read the following passages to see how that sort of betrayal affected the heart of King David. Then fill in the blanks below.

Even my close friend,

_____ — _____,

one who shared my bread,
    has turned against me.

PSALM 41:9

If an enemy were insulting me,
    I could endure it;
if a foe were rising against me,
    I could hide.

But it is you, a man like myself,
    my companion, my close friend,
with whom I once enjoyed _____ _____
    at the house of God,
as we walked about
    among the worshipers.

PSALM 55:12-14

Scholars believe it's very likely that the friend David is describing here is Ahithophel. They also believe David's words in these passages are messianic and prophetic. You'll recall two other friends who shared bread, sweet fellowship, and a relationship that spiraled into betrayal.

Turn to Matthew 26:20-26 and read how Jesus was betrayed by one of his closest friends. Describe what happened below.

Describe a time when you felt betrayed. Consider recent relationships as well as childhood experiences.

What does the Matthew 26 passage tell you about Jesus' ability to understand how you feel when you've been betrayed or rejected?

If you've been wounded deeply, you may feel as if you'll never be able to trust another soul again. In these moments, you will take one of two courses of action:

1. You will grow closer in a relationship of trust with God, the only one who is always faithful.
2. You will move further away from God, believing that no one is truly safe.

How have relationship betrayals affected your ability to trust other people?

How have those betrayals affected your ability to trust in God?

Scripture clearly speaks to how David and Jesus responded in the midst of their own betrayal. Let's learn from them as we seek to trust more in God.

Glance back at Psalm 55, which recounts David's deep dismay over the betrayal of his friend and counselor. Make special note of any words or phrases in verses 1-15 that hint at the depth of David's pain. Write them below.

Despite his pain, how does David end this psalm? Write the final sentence of Psalm 55:23 below:

Now let's see how Jesus responded after he made it clear that his friend Judas was about to betray him. Not long after Judas slunk off (John 13:27-30), Jesus delivered the following words to the remaining disciples: "Trust in God; trust also in me" (John 14:1). For emphasis, whom did Jesus say they should trust?

David and Jesus were familiar with your kind of pain. They understood rejection. They experienced circumstances that would have caused any one of us to think that God wasn't trustworthy. Yet their refrain through Scripture is this: Trust in God.

It's tempting to think, *Well, of course Jesus trusted God. He is part of the Trinity.* But David was one of us—a mere human.

What do the following passages—written by our brother David—reveal about the character of God? In each instance, how does the psalmist respond to God in light of who he is?

Those who know your name trust in you,
   for you, LORD, have never forsaken those who seek you.
PSALM 9:10

Some trust in chariots and some in horses,
    but we trust in the name of the LORD our God.

PSALM 20:7

In you, LORD my God,
    I put my trust.

PSALM 25:1

When I am afraid, I put my trust in you.

PSALM 56:3

Choose one verse from those listed above that reflects your trust in God—or that reflects your desire to trust in him. Write the verse on a piece of paper and hang it somewhere to remind you this week of God's trustworthiness. Memorize the verse so that it becomes a part of your thought patterns.

GETTING YOUR CONTROL UNDER CONTROL

We've spent time this week considering the trustworthiness of God because without building that relationship of trust, we will not be able to:

- turn over areas of unhealthy control to him
- surrender our plans to make certain they align with his
- recognize his voice
- do what he tells us to do
- learn when to hang on and when to let go

Earlier in this week's study, you did the hard work of evaluating your level of trust in God. Now it's time to broaden that trust so you can get your control under control. Friend, you will never know whether you can trust Jesus if you don't give him the chance to prove it. That's where the second *R* comes in: risk.

Our Bible is the resource that proves the risk is worth it. You can read all the self-help and Christian living books you want. But the only book that can transform your life is the Bible. The only person who can transform your heart is Jesus.

When we study God's Word, we can begin to trust his character, his control, and his mighty cross.

His character: Read the following verses. What do they reveal about God's character?

Deuteronomy 31:8

2 Samuel 7:28

Psalm 9:10

His control: Read the following verses. What comfort do they offer you as you consider handing over more control to God's trustworthy hands?

Deuteronomy 7:9

Isaiah 41:10

Luke 12:22-26

His cross: Read the following verses. What do they reveal about the power of the cross and the trustworthiness of the one who hung on it for you?

John 19:30

Colossians 1:20

1 Peter 2:24-25

We ask for a map, but instead Jesus gives us a compass and says, "Follow me."

During Jesus' time on earth, the Jewish people worshiped at the magnificent Temple in Jerusalem. The most hallowed place in the Temple was an inner room called the Holy of Holies. Only the high priest was allowed to enter the Holy of Holies, and that happened just once a year on Yom Kippur, when he offered a blood sacrifice "for the sins the people had committed" (Hebrews 9:7).

A thick veil separated the people from the Holy of Holies, and tradition indicates that the curtain was sixty feet high, thirty feet wide, and four inches thick. Because of this veil, the presence of God remained shielded from all people except for the high priest, who brought the sacrifice.

Yet the moment that Jesus cried out in a loud voice on the cross, giving up his spirit, a remarkable phenomenon occurred to that great veil separating people from God's presence: "At that moment the curtain of the temple was torn in two from top to bottom" (Matthew 27:51).

Underline the words in Matthew 27:51 that indicate that this tearing of the veil could only have come from God, not man.

That thick veil was torn top to bottom, a feat that no man could have accomplished. In an instant, the Holy of Holies was exposed. In an instant, people who were previously denied access to God could boldly enter his presence. In an instant, the high priest of the Temple was not the only one who could draw near to God. In an instant, the greatest High Priest of all made a way for us.

Read Hebrews 4:14-15 and write the name of that High Priest below.

Because of the work of our High Priest, who offered his own blood sacrifice, we have been given so many incredible gifts. One of those gifts is twenty-four-hour access to God.

> We can boldly enter heaven's Most Holy Place because of the blood of Jesus. By his death, Jesus opened a new and life-giving way through the curtain into the Most Holy Place. And since we have a great High Priest who rules over God's house, let us go right into the presence of God with sincere hearts fully trusting him.
>
> HEBREWS 10:19-22, NLT

Underline the words in Hebrews 10:19–22 that indicate how close you can get to God.

God wants you to enter right into his presence. There is no curtain. There is no veil. The only barriers between you and God . . . are the ones you put there yourself. God has invited you into an intimate relationship with him—a relationship "with sincere hearts fully trusting him."

Take the risk. Enter in. See God as a Father who desires intimacy with you.

God is holding out his hand and asking you to open yours today. Trust him with your plans. Trust him with your life. Because of his character, because of his control . . . *because of the cross.*

On Your Own

As you seek to trust God more in your daily life, use the Decision Tree as a practical tool to decide what to hang on to and what to let go. You can find it on page 108 or download it at www.ItsAllUnderControlBook.com /Resources.

It's All Under Control includes a story on pages 105–107 about letting go of imaginary balloons on which we've written names and words representing our concerns and our loved ones. Picture yourself grasping a bunch of balloons with names and words written on each one. As you do, take a few minutes to answer the questions to the right.

▶ What is written on your balloons?

▶ Are you hanging on because you're afraid of what will happen if you don't?

▶ Are you hanging on because you don't trust God as much as you trust yourself?

PRAYER

Let's pray with thanksgiving to this amazing High Priest who went before us with his own blood sacrifice, allowing us to draw near to God. Let's ask God for the strength to "boldly enter heaven's Most Holy Place"—all because of Jesus.

Write your prayer here.

WEEK 3
Wild Obedience

⋀⋀⋀⋀

This is love: that we walk in obedience to his commands.

2 JOHN 1:6

⋀⋀⋀⋀

WEEK 3 FOCUS

► To see how trusting God has Kingdom implications

► To concentrate more on obedience than desired outcomes

LET'S GET STARTED

Read chapters 7 and 8 of *It's All Under Control.*

For a bonus teaching video from Jennifer based on this week's session, visit www.ItsAllUnderControlBook.com/Resources.

LAST WEEK, we emphasized our access to God and his invitation to enter into a more intimate relationship with him. The more we get to know him, the more we will see that he is worthy of all our trust. We also talked about how risky that kind of relationship can feel.

This week, we will learn why trust is critically important as we let go of our need to control it all. Not only will trusting God change your life, but obedience to Jesus will produce fruit that may far outlive you! This will require you to take risks.

On a scale of 1 to 10 (1 being a total chicken, 10 being fearless), how big of a risk taker are you?

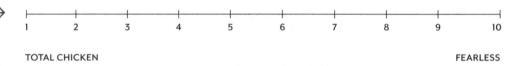

| 1 | 2 | 3 | 4 | 5 | 6 | 7 | 8 | 9 | 10 |

TOTAL CHICKEN   FEARLESS

This week, we will step out of comfort zones and learn this truth: The most meaningful moments happen when we take single steps of faith toward a trustworthy God. Of course, for those of us whose standard modus operandi is control, this can feel not only uncomfortable but dangerous.

MY STORY

Oh, friend, I'm not a very big risk taker. I prefer keeping everything under my control, rather than stepping out in blind faith. In fact, my idea of taking a big risk is trusting that my husband put down the toilet seat when I go to the bathroom in the middle of the night.

But God will ask us to take greater risks than that. These risks will require trust in him and a belief that his purposes are higher than ours. God will ask us to hand over control and follow him in obedience. This means we will have to let go of our agendas in favor of his. I talk about the difficulty of obedience in *It's All Under Control.*

> Obedience is not an act of the weak, but a rising up of the strong. Obedience might embarrass you or inconvenience you. Sometimes it will leave you in the dark, and the only light you will see is the small patch pooling at your feet. You ask for a spotlight to see straight ahead into the next two years of your life, but instead God gives you a "lamp unto [your] feet" and lets you see no further than this hour. (page 139)

Obedience requires that we surrender more than just our plans. We will have to surrender our approval ratings, our reputations, and our idealistic visions. This kind of obedience will ask us to exhibit farmer-style trust. Every spring, the whole countryside around my rural house kicks up its own dust as farmers push seeds below ground, into the dark. The farmer trusts that those tiny seeds will someday soon push against the earth with Herculean strength, busting forth with the fruit of a harvest.

In the same way, God asks us to plant seeds of obedience deep into the soil, trusting that he will grow something in his time.

Only when we know that God is working underneath the soil will we be willing to plant the seeds he has given us to sow. Pushing seeds down into the dark requires us to take a risk. And then we stand back and watch.

God grows. But first? We plant and wait.

YOUR STORY

When we live in obedience to God, what might happen to our misguided attempts to control outcomes?

Trust holds hands with obedience. Think of it this way. You are a first-time skydiver, thousands of feet in the air, and moments from jumping out of an airplane, your instructor takes you by the hand and says, "Trust me." Your instructor has a certain protocol so you don't kill yourself (or, if you're jumping tandem, so that you don't kill both of you).

I'm guessing you will obey the commands to take a flying leap *only* if you have come to trust your Instructor—because you checked out his credentials and track record and then completed training sessions with him.

Trusting God is similar. We won't obey our Instructor unless we trust him (which is why we put so much emphasis on trust in the previous lesson).

Think of a time when it felt as if God asked you to step out in wild obedience. Briefly describe that act of obedience. What happened? Describe the emotions you felt before, during, and after you stepped out in obedience.

As you reflect on your own act(s) of obedience, you likely remember your emotions. Perhaps you felt anxiety over the unknown. Perhaps you felt satisfaction in knowing you did what you'd been called to do. Maybe you felt disappointment because you didn't get to see the fruit from your obedience.

When you step out in trusting obedience to God, you let go of control. This is a scary-beautiful place to function as a human. Here you have no control over outcomes—not that you ever did.

But because we tend to live in the era of the "self-made" woman, we are lulled into believing that it's all on us. We pick our colleges, our cars, our neighborhoods, our churches, our jobs, our spouses, our parenting techniques. It's so easy to fall into patterns in which we become accidental gods of our own lives, thinking we're calling the shots. That's how the culture operates. But even though we live in a culture that gives us so many options that look like control, we are not called to live like the culture. If we love Jesus, we are called to lives of obedience instead.

Fill in the blanks to see how loving Jesus and obeying him go hand in hand for followers of Christ.

[Jesus said,] "If you love me, _____ ___ _____." (John 14:15)

[Jesus said,] "You are my friends if you do what I _____." (John 15:14)

This is _____: that we walk in _____ to his commands. (2 John 1:6)

Love and obedience. Look how the two walk side by side. Observe how God's Word links them together as sister virtues.

Take a moment to let the Holy Spirit speak to you about love and obedience. Do you sense that he is calling you into a fresh new season of obedience, flowing out of your love for him? Or do these verses affirm an area where you've been obedient in a recent season? If so, write what you're feeling.

Loving Jesus isn't about results. It's about obedience. Here's what I am learning about this kind of obedience. Most of the time, I really have no clue. For all the plans I've made, God continually delivers an invitation for me to let go of my plans in favor of his. He doesn't give me a map with all the roads clearly marked. Instead he gives me a compass to guide me in the general direction.

> Obedience does not always offer [instant] gratification. Instead, obedience requires an eternal perspective because we may never see the results here on earth. (*It's All Under Control*, page 145)

What is one thing you sense God may be calling you to do in obedience?

How do you respond to the idea that you might not see the results in your lifetime?

THEIR STORY

God must have known how scary it is to step out in faith because he shows us repeatedly on the pages of Scripture how it's done.

Those stories have given me the courage I needed to step out in faith. Did you know that I was an agnostic for many years? Yep. The woman who is leading you on this journey used to put Jesus in the same category as comic-book superheroes: strong and mighty on paper, but pure fiction and utterly useless in time of need.

I remained faithless until I responded to a strong sense, thumping inside of me, that I finally needed to do three things: tell someone about the depth of my doubt, search the Scriptures for answers, and actually pray about my unbelief. I didn't know until later that the nudge compelling me to do those three things was the Holy Spirit.

If you would have told me back then that I would have a speaking and writing ministry for Jesus, I would have told you that you were crazy!

Only God.

It took me a long time to muster up the courage to trust an unseen God and then to follow him into the wild realm of obedience. One of the ways I gained the confidence to step out in faithful obedience was by examining the stories of other people who responded to Jesus when he asked them to do remarkable, and sometimes seemingly ridiculous, things.

Let's meet some of those people.

Read the following Bible stories and fill in the chart with brief answers. Pay particular attention to the commands that Jesus gave people. Also, put yourself in the shoes of the Bible characters and imagine how you would have felt if you were the one being called to take that step of faith. Consider the doubts, fears, and uncertainties you would have had in regard to what he was asking you to do.

	WATER TO WINE JOHN 2:1-10	THE HEALING AT THE POOL JOHN 5:1-15	BLIND MAN HEALED JOHN 9:1-7
What problem needed Jesus' attention?			
What command did Jesus give to people immediately before the miracle?			
How would you have reacted to this command?			
What was the result?			

Review your responses to the question: "What command did Jesus give to the people immediately before the miracle?"

You probably gave answers such as:

"Fill the jars."

"Get up."

"Go, wash."

*When we stop trying to be Jesus,
the astonishing result is
that we actually become
more like him.*

Do you see how each of these miracles began with a single step of faith? Each person was asked to do something pretty outrageous.

In the chart, I asked how you would have reacted to Jesus' commands. Let me be completely honest with you. If Jesus had asked me to fill ceremonial jars with water, I would have secretly thought he had lost his mind. If I had been a paralytic for thirty-eight years when Jesus saw me by that pool, I would have doubted that I could "get up." And as the blind man, I might have wondered what good it would do to "go wash" to receive my sight. Couldn't Jesus have saved a little bit of time and energy by skipping over seemingly superfluous steps? In each of these situations, Jesus could have simply snapped his fingers to make a miracle. But each time, the person on the receiving end of the miracle *had to respond to the command of Jesus.* They had to release control over their lives (as little and as pitiful as that control might have seemed) and risk obeying Jesus.

As the saying goes, "You can't walk on water if you don't get out of the boat." Jesus is calling us out onto the water too: "Come." How will we respond?

In Jesus' first miracle, we see his amazing power on display. But don't overlook the great advice Mary offered—advice relevant to each of us today. Read John 2:5 and write the five words of instruction from Mary.

Here's how we can apply that five-word instruction in our everyday lives.

"Do whatever he tells you." Ask the Lord every day for your instructions.

"Do whatever he tells you." Say yes to the invitation to partner with him.

"Do whatever he tells you." No matter the task, the assignment, the deadline. Ask him to guide you, and then obey his commands.

"Do whatever he tells you." Become so intimately familiar with the voice of Jesus that you can recognize it. Then say yes to whatever crazy, wonderful, unexpected, wacky thing he's asking you to do.

You don't know what will come of your wild obedience, but Jesus does. He knows how to turn your water into wine. (*It's All Under Control*, page 129)

Friend, as we let go of control, let's listen to Mary's words in our ears today: "Do whatever he tells you." Let's take the first step in wild obedience. Because that's where the miracle begins.

Mary's words would also have been appropriate for leaders of the early church, to whom God sometimes gave audacious assignments. One of my favorite acts of wild obedience happened in those early days of the church. Meet our friend Ananias. The Lord spoke to him in a vision and asked him to do something that sounded foolhardy.

Read Acts 9:11-12. Whom does the Lord want Ananias to call on?

Yes, *that* Saul. The one who was notorious for persecuting Christians. The one who wanted to arrest every Christian he could find and bring them back to Jerusalem in chains. The one who was "breathing out murderous threats against the Lord's disciples" (Acts 9:1). Read a bit more about Saul in Acts 9:3-9 and briefly describe what happened to him.

Enter Ananias. He had heard about the notorious Saul, and who can blame him if he felt a bit of knee-knocking trepidation in obeying the Lord? I can imagine Ananias's voice shaking as he spoke these words: "Lord . . . I have heard many reports about this man and all the harm he has done to your holy people in Jerusalem. And he has come here with authority from the chief priests to arrest all who call on your name" (Acts 9:13-14).

But the Lord isn't playing. "Go!" he says (verse 15). Note the exclamation mark.

Think for a moment how you would have reacted if the Lord asked you to put your life on the line. Or perhaps you've already faced a terrifying situation in which God called you to "Go!"

Describe your feelings and/or the situation here.

I can relate to Ananias. I can relate to the dread. The wavering trust. The fear. How often have I said, in my own way, to God: "Are you sure?" To which God replies, "Go!"

And that's exactly what Ananias did. He went.

Read Acts 9:17-22. Answer the following questions.

What did Ananias call Saul (Acts 9:17)?

What does this greeting tell us about Ananias's trust in God?

What happened as a result of Ananias's wild obedience to the command "Go!" (Acts 9:22)?

"Do whatever he tells you." And that's exactly what Ananias did. Despite every fear. Despite every potential doubt. Despite all of the "Who, me?" questions that plague people all the time. As a result of Ananias's obedience, Saul—whom we also know as Paul—became one of the most influential leaders in the history of Christianity. That plan was set in motion when one man fearlessly responded to the call: "Go!"

Someday when I get to heaven, I am going to ask Ananias if he was scared. I'm guessing he'll tell me something like this: "Yes, I was scared! But you know what's even scarier? Disobeying the God of the universe and deciding to go your way instead."

GETTING YOUR CONTROL UNDER CONTROL

As we work to get our control under control, we'll find that the more we trust God, the more we can hear his voice. The more we can hear his voice, the more often we'll hear him telling us to go. Or to wait. Or to stay. Or to run.

Reread the five-word instruction from Mary: "Do whatever he tells you." Next, go back to the list on page 5 where we identified areas of unhealthy control, which you marked with an X. Take a few moments to prayerfully consider whether God wants you to take a step of wild obedience in any of those areas today. (For example, if you marked "what people think of me," listen for ways

On Your Own

This week, take God off your to-do list and instead write a list that puts God in charge of the agenda. As you sit at the kitchen table or your desk each morning, tune in to God's plans for your day by praying over verses like:

Do whatever he tells you.
JOHN 2:5

Whatever you do, do it all for the glory of God.
1 CORINTHIANS 10:31

When you're finished, you'll have created a daily to-do list under the direct supervision of God. Don't stress yourself out if you don't feel like you had a clear indication of what God wants you to do every day. Instead, repeatedly remind yourself that he's with you as you go about your daily tasks.

that God might want you to take a step that could put your approval rating in jeopardy.)

Now write down the area or areas from that list where you need God's direction today in regard to obedience.

If you sense God asking you to step into a place of wild—or even mild—obedience, circle the word that best describes God's whispers to you today. Or feel free to write your own word in the margin.[*]

Go   Wait   Stay   Run   Kneel   Return   Believe   Worship

When you are called into obedience, what holds you back?

---

[*] Note: If you don't have clarity on this, please feel free to skip this exercise and return to it later.

One reason obedience is so scary is that we don't know what will come of it. In fact, you may feel like some of your most obedient acts resulted in failure. Can you think of things you've done out of obedience in the past that haven't yet shown any fruit? Explain.

When that happens—and there's a good chance you will experience this if you haven't already—remember this: The most important work you ever do might outlive you. If God called you, he had a reason. If you've been obedient, you haven't really failed at all; you've been faithful.

Friend, let's believe it together: The Holy Spirit is working in the silences.

Our main job is not to manage outcomes. It is simply to show up. Everything else is up to God. We cannot always see "everything else." But someday, I believe, we will. (*It's All Under Control*, page 147)

PRAYER

Not long ago, I realized how much I needed the Holy Spirit's power to live in obedience to Christ. I shared that prayer in *It's All Under Control*, and I do so here as well. As we take our wild obedience to the next level of trust, let's pray that prayer together. Underline any passages in this prayer (page 56) that you especially want to pray to the Holy Spirit, based on what's happening in your life right now. In your own words, add a few lines to the prayer in the space provided on the next page.

Dear Holy Spirit,

    I don't always pray to you. Maybe it's because you're harder to wrap my mind around. I "get" a Father. I relate to the person of Jesus. But, Holy Spirit, you are wind and wandering and wild. You are breath. You come and go as you please, and sometimes you light upon my skin like a flame. You are presence, and you are power. I look back on my life and see startling evidence of your fingerprints; those are always the weak-kneed moments that make me go, "Whoa."

    You were present at Creation, hovering over the waters, and you haven't left us since. You come to us through water and Word, bread and wine. I find you at the altar—and on the floor. I find you in my deepest joys and lingering around the edges of my heart when the pain is too much.

    You kind of scare me because you remind me that my self-sufficiency is worth nothing when you're around. You like me weak, and I don't do weak well. You like me needy, and I don't do needy well. You never once let me be the hero. I am always the rescued. You are the helper, the counselor, the reassuring hand upon my back when I would have sworn to you that I was the only one in the room. When I neglect you, I'm like a candle without a flame.

    You don't just bring the fire. You are the fire. You cause me to jump when I want to hide. You make me to run free when I want to walk away.

    Holy Spirit, don't let me ever take another step in this life without checking in with you first—and surrendering myself wholly to you.

_____

_____

_____

_____

Holy Spirit, you are welcome here. Amen.[1]

Why You Need Help
(and the Courage to Ask for It)

⋀⋀⋀⋀

I am the LORD your God
who takes hold of your right hand
and says to you, Do not fear;
I will help you.

ISAIAH 41:13

⋀⋀⋀⋀

WEEK 4 FOCUS

▸ To gain the courage to delegate and ask for help

▸ To consider practical ways to say no, even if it means disappointing people

LET'S GET STARTED

Read chapters 9 and 10 of *It's All Under Control.*

For a bonus teaching video from Jennifer based on this week's session, visit www.ItsAllUnderControlBook.com/Resources.

LAST WEEK, we gained a fresh understanding of how trusting God has Kingdom implications. When we trust and obey him, we may produce fruit that will far outlive us.

This week, we will address one of the signs that we're trying to control too much: busyness. Perhaps you are the kind of woman others view as responsible, which means you are actually *asked* to take control of a lot in your community, job, or family. Others depend on you. (You probably know the saying "If you want something done, ask a busy woman to do it.") But you've come to realize that you simply can't do it all. Yet how do you let go? We keep adding more to our lists for the following five reasons:

1. *I'm capable; therefore, I should.*
2. *It's the right thing to do.*
3. *If I don't do it, no one else will.*
4. *If someone else does it, it won't be done properly.*
5. *I don't want to disappoint others.*

Which of the above thoughts resonate with you? Circle all that apply. Feel free to add your own reasons in the margin.

Mark on the scale below how overwhelmed you feel by all that's on your plate now.

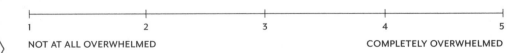

1	2	3	4	5

NOT AT ALL OVERWHELMED   COMPLETELY OVERWHELMED

We have to face some tough realities when we begin to look at our busy lives. There are some things we love that we'll simply have to let go of. There are people we will disappoint when we tell them no. And there is the hard work of asking for help, which doesn't happen naturally for a lot of us. The good news: Jesus knew we'd struggle. The even better news: He shows us how to work through that struggle.

This week, let's learn directly from Jesus how to: ask for help, say no, and accept the fact that we will sometimes disappoint people.

MY STORY

Let me confess that I tend to take on far more than I should. I circled all five of the reasons listed on page 58. Clearly so much of what we're called to do we can't simply opt out of. But we need to carefully evaluate everything on our agenda to make sure it aligns with God's. I generally have a high tolerance for heavy workloads, but just because I *can* doesn't mean I *should*.

Here's how I know when I've gone too far. When I get so overwhelmed with busyness that my spiritual growth stagnates, that's a huge red flag. God will never ask you or me to stretch ourselves so thin that we don't have time for him.

That's where the "Do, Delegate, or Dismiss" technique, which I unpack in chapter 9 of *It's All Under Control*, comes into play. With this strategy, I listen for God's direction on what to do, what to delegate, and what to simply dismiss. And then when I sense God's leading, I must do what was spelled out in last week's lesson: I have to be obedient to his direction.

Obedience means that I will likely have to say no to many opportunities, thus disappointing someone who has relied on me in the past. Disappointing someone can feel shameful.

Obedience also means that I might have to accept help. I'm terrible at asking for help. I'd rather be the helper instead of the helped. I don't like feeling needy.

Asking for help requires a stripped-down vulnerability. When we ask for help, we are moving closer to an intimacy with people that feels a little dangerous. (*It's All Under Control*, page 171)

YOUR STORY

Are there certain areas where you feel particularly overwhelmed but reluctant to say no or to ask for help? Check all the areas that apply below.

☐ Work
☐ Household duties
☐ Children
☐ Relationships
☐ Volunteer roles
☐ Church commitments
☐ Other _____

Put a check beside any of the statements below that resonate with your experience.

☐ I have corners of my life where I don't let people in because I'm afraid they'll mess things up.
☐ I don't like asking for help because it makes me feel needy or weak.
☐ I don't ask for help unless it's as a last resort.
☐ I don't ask for help because I'm afraid of being told no.
☐ Collaboration sounds like more trouble than it's worth.
☐ I've asked for help before, and people have let me down.
☐ I feel guilty if I tell someone no.
☐ I sometimes say yes to things I shouldn't because I don't want to disappoint someone.
☐ Other _____

When we're stretched too thin and unwilling to ask for help, our relationships may suffer most—including our relationship with the Lord. Often one sign that I'm too busy is feeling distant from God. As I shared earlier in this week's study, when I get too busy trying to control too much, my spiritual growth is stagnant. *God will never ask us to stretch ourselves so thin that we don't have time for him.*

How do you react to that last statement? How does busyness affect your relationship with God?

When we refuse to say no or ask for help, we face unwanted consequences. Here are a few: feeling distant from God, feeling resentful toward others, feeling burned out and weary. Sound familiar?

As you examine your own life, put yourself in Moses' shoes for a moment. Imagine that, like Moses, you are a leader being pulled in a lot of directions. You've got much work to do, but the needs of others are piling up on you. Some of those needs and requests might be keeping you from doing what God actually called you to do. We see that scenario playing out for Moses on a day when he was serving as a judge for the Hebrew people. Moses had a lot of other tasks on his agenda, but that day, he took a seat before his people. Imagine the line of people, snaking out the door and around the corner. According to Scripture, there were so many Hebrews demanding time with Moses that their complaints consumed his entire workday. "They stood around him from morning till evening" (Exodus 18:13). Now imagine that when he headed back to his tent for the night, everything God had *actually* asked him to do had been left undone on account of all the demands placed on him by all of those people.

Moses' father-in-law, Jethro, saw the whole thing play out, and he knew that Moses needed a talking-to. Read this exchange between Moses and his father-in-law. Underline the parts that strike a chord in you.

When Moses' father-in-law saw all that he was doing for the people, he said, "What's going on here? Why are you doing all this, and all by yourself, letting everybody line up before you from morning to night?"

Moses said to his father-in-law, "Because the people come to me with questions about God. When something comes up, they come to me. I judge between a man and his neighbor and teach them God's laws and instructions."

Moses' father-in-law said, "This is no way to go about it. You'll burn out, and the people right along with you. This is way too much for you—you can't do this alone. Now listen to me. Let me tell you how to do this so that God will be in this with you."

EXODUS 18:14-19, MSG

Circle the passage above where Moses justifies why he put too much on his plate. When have you felt that same way?

His father-in-law went on to remind Moses what his actual job was. Moses was called to show his people how to live and what to do. And then Jethro gave Moses fantastic advice: Delegate to competent people who could help share the load. Here's why: "If you handle the work this way, you'll have the strength to carry out whatever God commands you" (Exodus 18:23, MSG).

What light does this shed on your life and all that you feel you need to be "in control of" these days?

Sometimes when we are extremely busy, we don't stop to listen to others' offers of help or words of wisdom. Who might be trying to play the role of Jethro in your life? What advice might you take from them?

THEIR STORY

We got a jump start on our biblical application by reflecting on what Moses learned about delegating and saying no. Now we'll jump ahead to the Gospels, where Jesus provides some rich lessons on what it looks like to ask for help and what it looks like to disappoint people.

Yes, even Jesus asked for help.

And yes, even Jesus—Savior of the world—disappointed people.

Let's dig in and find out more.

Read the following Bible passages and describe what Jesus asked other people to do.

Matthew 14:16-20

Mark 14:32-34

Luke 22:7-13

John 4:7

John 19:26-27

In each scenario, Jesus asked for help.

He asked for a drink of water. For assistance as he provided a miracle feast. For his disciples to prepare the upper room. For his dearest friends to keep watch as his soul ached with sorrow. For someone to take care of his mother.

Why do you think Jesus asked for help?

Scripture reveals that Jesus was both fully God and fully man. Because of his divinity, he could have handled any of the above situations on his own. But because he was human, he entered fully into every condition we face, including our condition of needing help.

Read Hebrews 2:17-18 to see how much Jesus understands how you feel right now. How human was Jesus, according to those verses?

In *The Message*, these verses say that Jesus "experienced it all himself—all the pain, all the testing—and would be able to help where help was needed" (Hebrews 2:18).

Furthermore, Jesus shows us that God can do for us what we cannot do on our own. Even Jesus prayed for God to help him do what he came to do (see Mark 14:35; John 17:1-5).

What reassurance does this knowledge about Jesus asking for help give you?

Read Isaiah 41:13. What does this verse suggest about God's willingness to help when you call on him?

> When you ask for help—from people and from God—you are not weak. The truth is, you are now strong enough to admit that you can't face your problems on your own. (*It's All Under Control*, page 172)

We've established that Jesus asked for help. But how about my assertion that Jesus disappointed people? Maybe you're wondering what I'm basing that on. Let's return to the Gospels to find out.

Read the following Bible passages and think about the ways Jesus may have disappointed people in each of the stories. Write any observations you have.

Mark 1:35-38

Mark 2:15-16

John 11:17-23

Yep. Even Jesus disappointed people. Instead of sticking around Simon's neighborhood, he moved on to another village (Mark 1:35-38). He disappointed religious leaders when he dined with sinners (Mark 2:16). He showed up late for a medical house call, arriving after the funeral was over (John 11:21).

Jesus even disappointed his own family, who questioned his mental stability. Once when a huge crowd had gathered in a home to hear Jesus speak, he and his disciples weren't even able to find time to eat. "When his family heard about this, they went to take charge of him, for they said, 'He is out of his mind'" (Mark 3:21).

Bravery is letting go when you want to hang on.

Believe me. I know how hard it is to disappoint people. I have a bad history of piling on more duties because my sense of duty convinces me that I have to say yes. At times in my life, I haven't been able to imagine not meeting everyone's expectations. But we all have limits—even Jesus. Even you.

So often we think that the best way to love people is to do whatever they want us to do. But that's not true. The best way to love is *to do only what God has called you to do*.

How does this revelation help you gain perspective on your limitations and your calling?

GETTING YOUR CONTROL UNDER CONTROL

At the beginning of this week's study, I promised you that we would learn some practical steps to say no, even if it means disappointing people. Only then will we truly be able to focus on God's best for our lives and let him take control of areas where we are reluctant to let go.

Prayerfully consider an area where you have sensed—now or in the past—that God wanted you to say no, yet you feared disappointing someone. Describe the scenario and the outcomes.

Maybe you feel as if God is prompting you to say no in this current season. Or maybe you missed that chance. If so, that's okay. Hindsight is a terrific teacher. Let's commit to not repeating our past mistakes. Let's commit to saying no when we should, without guilt or shame.

In chapter 9 of *It's All Under Control*, I offer six steps you can take to dismiss what needs to be dismissed. Each one offers a practical step to help you say no. Read each one.

1. **Know who you are.** When you have a clear sense of your purpose and identity in Christ, you'll be able to say no without letting it prescribe something about your worth. Take time every day to affirm your truest identity in Jesus.

2. **Know your priorities.** Filter every request for your time through the prism of your core boundaries, values, and calling.

3. **Be resolute.** As Jesus said, "All you need to say is simply 'Yes' or 'No'" (Matthew 5:37).

4. **Keep perspective.** Remember that a yes to one more thing means a no to something else.

5. **Remind yourself that your no is someone else's yes.** Your no may open the door for another soul to learn, lead, and serve.

6. **Hear God's big yes over you.** Hear these words from Paul: "Whatever God has promised gets stamped with the Yes of Jesus. . . . God affirms us, making us a sure thing in Christ, putting his Yes within us" (2 Corinthians 1:20-22, MSG).

Which one resonates most with you? Explain.

On Your Own

Have you been asked to take on a new responsibility at church, your kids' school, or in the community? Or do you feel overwhelmed by everything already on your plate? To help you decide whether to "Do, Delegate, or Dismiss" a particular task, I have created a flowchart, which is available on page 109 or available for download at www.ItsAllUnderControlBook.com/Resources.

Try running a task-related decision through the chart.

One way to learn to say no is to practice when the stakes aren't high, such as when a cashier asks you to provide your e-mail address for a store's weekly ads. If you're like me, you might intend to say no, but in the process get tongue-tied, and end up agreeing to one more thing.

Perhaps you simply need practice saying no. One way to do so is by using the word *don't* instead of *can't*. We think the two words are interchangeable, but psychologically, they are quite different. Consider the difference between these two:

- ▸ "I can't take on one more committee position, so I am going to decline this time."
- ▸ "I don't take more than two volunteer positions a year, and I am already at my max, so my answer is no."

How you say no matters.

The *can't* phrase implies a restriction by an outside force, and some may think your no is up for negotiation. The *don't* phrase is empowering and shows your determination to make the best choices for your life.

In the space provided, write your own script that will help you say no when someone asks you to take something that isn't yours to handle. Consider including the word *don't* to demonstrate the healthy limits you have for your life.

PRAYER

Take a deep breath. Feel the relief that comes with knowing that it's not all up to you. Enjoy the freedom that comes in establishing ground rules for yourself. Yes, you might disappoint someone with your no. But when you say no, you'll be able to shine brighter in what God has actually called you to do.

Let's pray that God will give us the strength to learn when to ask for help and when to say no to that which he never asked us to control.

Dear Lord,

I want to live for your agenda, your purposes, your plans, and your call. Give me the strength to let go of what you have not asked me to do, so I can shine at what you have. Then give me the courage to say yes to your plans and no to everything else. And give me the wisdom to know the difference. Today I especially need help discerning how to deal with:

_____

_____

_____

_____

In Jesus' name, amen.

The Permission You Need to Rest

〰〰

Come with me by yourselves to a quiet place and get some rest.

MARK 6:31

〰〰

WEEK 5 FOCUS

▸ To work toward a healthier view of rest

▸ To exchange our drive for control with a desire for calm

LET'S GET STARTED

Read chapters 11, 12, and 13 of *It's All Under Control*.

For a bonus teaching video from Jennifer based on this week's session, visit www.ItsAllUnderControlBook.com/Resources.

I HOPE YOU FOUND SOME RELIEF as you worked through the previous session. As you begin to put the lesson into practice, long-needed margin in your life will emerge. However, because you are a dependable, capable woman, you will likely be tempted to fill those freed-up spaces with new assignments. May you find the courage to *resist* in times when God is calling you to *rest*.

This week, we will learn the importance of rest and stillness.

How do those two words—*rest* and *stillness*—make you feel? Select the answer that best describes your viewpoint right now.

    a. peaceful, because I know the value of rest

    b. yearning, because I long to rest but don't know how

    c. antsy, because I don't like being still

    d. guilty, because I have not rested like I ought to

    e. _____ [Fill in the blank with a word of your choosing.]

No matter where you are today, I believe that God has a message intended just for you in this week's lesson.

MY STORY

When it comes to rest, I have felt all those things: peaceful, yearning, antsy, and guilty. Let me confess to you that I have not been the best at resting and waiting. After all, I am most comfortable when I feel on top of all the details. One of my dear friends knows this about me, and several years ago, she sent me a text with a quote from Charles Spurgeon:

"Stand still;" keep the posture of an upright man, ready for action, expecting further orders, cheerfully and patiently awaiting the directing voice; and it will not be long before God shall say to you, as distinctly as Moses said it to the people of Israel, "Go forward."[2]

My friend knew it. Spurgeon knew it. The Scriptures are very clear about it: Wait on the Lord.

Wait. Not run ahead, or manage outcomes for God. Simply wait, and as you wait, you rest. But let me get honest with you. I laughed out loud when I first read that Spurgeon quote. Unlike Spurgeon, I've found waiting to be neither a cheerful experience nor one that inspires patience.

In *It's All Under Control*, I confess one reason why I'm not naturally good at waiting:

Waiting makes me feel powerless and sometimes hopeless. But God is teaching me something very important about waiting with my unmet longings: While we're waiting, God is working. (page 187)

No, I'm not naturally good at waiting, which for me, means I'm also not very good at resting. Resting feels risky. Why? If I'm resting, I might have to feel things I don't want to feel. For me, work can become something like a culturally acceptable drug—a distraction of sorts, so I don't have to deal with the hard stuff in my life.

God has been training my heart to hear his quiet whispers. Has he been doing the same thing for you? Nothing else will change us quite like the voice of the Lord, who rummages around in our souls to uproot lies and replant truth.

When I get off course, his voice is the one thing that gets me back on track. "Listen for God's voice in everything you do, everywhere you go; he's the one who will *keep you on track*" (Proverbs 3:6, MSG, emphasis added).

The trouble is, we can get so busy, so distracted, so overloaded with obligations that we can't hear the voice of God. This week's lesson is about rest so that we can hear, at last, the peaceful voice of the Lord. Rather than constantly striving, we can be at peace in the midst of silence and quietness. Let's pray that God will help us exchange our drive for control with a desire for calm.

Dear God, never let me get so busy that I can't hear your voice. Help me to rest so I can hear you speak to my heart. Let me give control over to you, and in exchange, I receive your calm reassurance. Amen.

Let go of what God has not asked you to do, so you can shine at what he has.

YOUR STORY

How do you make time for regular rest? If you don't, what are the biggest obstacles to rest in your life?

Are there certain days or times of the day when you find yourself most able to rest?

Are there any particular Bible verses, songs, images, or places that evoke a sense of rest and peace for you?

One of the best-known Bible passages is the Twenty-third Psalm. It is filled with rich imagery of restfulness. Before we move on, spend some time meditating on this passage. Because some of the older translations of Psalm 23 have become so familiar to us, let's read a version that may be less familiar—Eugene Peterson's paraphrase. I urge you to move slowly through these words, pausing after each line to visualize the scene. Underline anything that evokes strong visual images of rest for you. Consider this exercise an opportunity to practice rest, even as you read!

> GOD, my shepherd!
>   I don't need a thing.
> You have bedded me down in lush meadows,
>   you find me quiet pools to drink from.
> True to your word,
>   you let me catch my breath
>   and send me in the right direction.
> Even when the way goes through
>   Death Valley,
> I'm not afraid
>   when you walk at my side.
> Your trusty shepherd's crook
>   makes me feel secure.
> You serve me a six-course dinner
>   right in front of my enemies.
> You revive my drooping head;
>   my cup brims with blessing.

Your beauty and love chase after me
    every day of my life.
I'm back home in the house of GOD
    for the rest of my life.

PSALM 23:1-6, MSG

Look again at the phrases you underlined. Why did you choose those sections?

Now I'm going to ask you to do something that might feel a little weird. But I believe this exercise may help you slow down and grab hold of God's promise of rest. Here it is:

Even if you don't consider yourself an artist, take a few moments to dwell on one of the phrases you underlined. Then draw a representation of that image on page 79. As you draw, listen to a song or two from your radio or iTunes library that evokes peacefulness. Allow yourself to sink into the Twenty-third Psalm mentally and spiritually. (If you are intimidated by a drawing exercise, please know that stick figures are fine! This isn't an art contest; rather, it's an intentional exercise to slow down and sink into God's beautiful promises. Plus, if you are doing this Bible study with a group, your drawing might make for a bit of entertainment.)

Keep that feeling of peacefulness in your mind as you continue to progress through this week's study. Rest is not out of reach. God is calling you into true rest, not only when you get to heaven but—as verse 6 suggests—"every day of [your] life."

THEIR STORY

We've spent time with several of our spiritual ancestors over the last few weeks. Now let's go back and reacquaint ourselves with our very first spiritual ancestors: Adam and Eve. They have an important lesson for us about rest.

Skim through Genesis 1 and make a mental note of all that happened on days one through six.

Fill out this timeline with the main event of each day.

Day 1 _____

Day 2 _____

Day 3 _____

Day 4 _____

Day 5 _____

Day 6 _____

Next make note of what God did on the seventh day. (Read Genesis 2:3 and fill in the blanks.)

Then God blessed the _____ ____ and made it holy, because on it he _____ _____ ___ ___ _____ of creating that he had done.

Most likely, this story is very familiar to you, even if you didn't grow up in the church or the Christian faith. We know that God rested on the seventh day after he completed the most comprehensive creative act in the history of forever. Yep, even the Lord of the universe thought it wise to rest.

But what I want you to notice here is something that often gets overlooked. Sure, we all know that God rested after his six days of work. But let's take a moment to consider when this day of rest came for Adam and Eve.

I'm about to make a key point regarding rest. To help it sink in, write down the day of the week (1–7) on which Adam and Eve were created. Day _____

Which day (1–7) was appointed as the day of rest? Day _____

How many days were Adam and Eve on the earth before that day of rest came?

This is what I see: Adam and Eve's day of rest came within twenty-four hours of their time on earth. Rest came before they worked the land. Rest came before they clocked in at the office. Rest came before they tidied up the house. For God, rest came on the seventh day. But for these first two humans, resting happened on their *first full day* on earth. Rest happened *before* the work, not after it!

GETTING YOUR CONTROL UNDER CONTROL

I've gotten it all backwards. I tend to rest *after* my work is done. I rest at 7:30 p.m. on the couch, but only *after* the dishes are washed and put away. I rest on Sunday *after* a long week of work. That doesn't sound so terribly wrong or unbiblical, does it? But God has surprised me with a brand-new revelation: I was designed to rest *first*, so that my work can flow out of my rest.

How does that last statement strike you?

Have you tended to view rest as something that comes before the work or after the work?

I share some of my thoughts about work and rest in *It's All Under Control*: "Rest has often looked like hitting the wall, tank on empty, with nothing left except the satisfaction of a job well done. I don't think that's what God intended. . . . I wasn't designed to rest *last*. I was designed to rest *first*, so that my work would flow out of rest" (pages 219–220).

I accidentally put this rest-before-work theory to the test in 2016, right before launching the biggest writing project of my life up to that point. My book *The Happiness Dare* was scheduled to release on a Tuesday in August. The weekend before the book released, there was plenty of work I could have done to prepare for the launch, enough tasks that could have kept me busy around the clock.

But I didn't work that weekend. I went to the lake with my family and spent most of my waking hours in a lounge chair near the shore while reading a book called *Rhythms of Rest* by Shelly Miller. The book beautifully illustrates how busy people can make rest a reality. She writes that the constant pressure of unfinished work is why people don't rest.

If we use unfinished work as an excuse, however, we will never rest, she says. That's because our work is never really finished. Shelly writes:

On the sixth day, God didn't say, "I'm finished"—full stop—as a justification for a day of rest on the seventh. God is in the business of continually creating, and his work is never fully finished. The work you have to do while you are on this earth is never fully finished either.[3]

There will always be unfinished work. Don't let it be a reason not to rest, or you never will.

Can you think of a way to apply the "rest first" principle this week? Does that feel like a challenging, unrealistic concept? What is one area where you could attempt to put it into practice?

As someone who prefers to be running on all cylinders, feeling as if everything is humming and under control, rest can seem like a luxury I can't afford. Yet I've learned that when I'm short on rest, I look like anything but a controlled woman. Instead I forget things and tend to withdraw. I become irritable, prone to tearful outbursts, and short with the people I love.

What warning signs indicate you are short on rest?

On Your Own

This week try one or two of these helpful tips to incorporate more rest into your life:

▶ *Instead of scrolling, go strolling.* Contrary to popular opinion, checking social media does not always count as rest. Rather than scrolling through Instagram after dinner, try taking a walk instead.

▶ *Don't let your "yes" encroach on your rest.* When you agree to something new, let something else go before sacrificing time you could be using for needed rest.

▶ *Let your work assignments flow from soul realignments.* Remember that rest is essential to hear clear directions so that our souls and agendas are aligned.

▶ *Protect the freed-up time you have already created.* Rather than filling up time with more activity, protect your downtime. It will make you more productive in the work you were designed to do.

▶ *What others would you add?*

When you see those danger signs in your life, take a moment to consider if you are rest deprived. And then make rest a priority, no matter how much you need to do. I know what you might be thinking: *But, Jennifer. I'm just too busy.* While it's true that there are seasons in which rest is an elusive dream, the busiest man I know found time to rest. That man was Jesus of Nazareth.

During his time on earth, the work was always unfinished. There was always another person who needed healing, another demon that needed to be cast out, another crowd that needed food, another group that needed to be taught, another sinner who needed hope. But no matter how busy Jesus was, he knew the importance of rest, and he invited his closest friends to rest as well.

Read Mark 6:30-31. What words did Jesus speak to the disciples? Write those words in the space below, and as you write, hear these words as an invitation to you.

Dear friend, if Jesus needed to stop and rest, so do you. The good news is, you have his permission—as well as his personal invitation—to rest.

PRAYER

Dear Jesus,

If even you needed rest, then I do too. As the demands of this world press in, remind me to take time to replenish my tired soul and body. In your Word, you invite all who are weary and burdened into a place of rest (Matthew 11:28-29). Thank you for this invitation. Give me the strength to say yes to rest, even though the day's work is unfinished. In your name I pray, amen.

Under the Control of God Alone

〰〰〰〰

You, however, are not in the realm of the flesh but are in the realm
of the Spirit, if indeed the Spirit of God lives in you.

ROMANS 8:9

〰〰〰〰

WEEK 6 FOCUS

▸ To gain a clearer understanding of what it means to live a self-controlled life

▸ To recognize the source of our self-control

LET'S GET STARTED

Read chapter 14 of *It's All Under Control.*

For a bonus teaching video from Jennifer based on this week's session, visit www.ItsAllUnderControlBook.com/Resources.

LAST WEEK, we were challenged to make rest a higher priority in our lives.

Were you able to take time for rest this week? Share something about how you incorporated rest into your week.

MY STORY

You did it! You persevered and made it to the end of this study. Together we've learned when to let go and when to hang on tighter than ever before. We've learned to ask for help and to delegate. We've learned when to say yes and when to say no, even though we know we'll disappoint people. We also cracked the control code. When I asked you to crack that code, I was cracking it myself. Like I said in the book, I was one tough nut to crack! Yet as I wrote in *It's All Under Control*:

> This is the rock-bottom truth: You will never regret time spent with Jesus. And you will never regret a decision to trust God. (page 236)

Despite all the ways in which we've grown, friend, we're not done yet. We've got a little more work to do. We've spent a whole book and Bible study exploring issues related to control, so it seems fitting to close our time together talking about self-control.

Here are a few of my thoughts on this subject:

I used to think that self-control was simply about not indulging in our desires. . . .

Turns out, self-control is so much bigger than that. . . . Self-control is actually *God's* control at work in us. *Strong's Concordance* defines *self-control* as something "proceeding out from *within* oneself, but not *by* oneself."[4] Which means that we don't do this in our own power. The Greek word for self-control is *enkráteia*, which means "true mastery from within." For the believer, this kind of self-control can only happen by the power of God working within us. (*It's All Under Control*, pages 245–246)

I have long looked at self-control as just another way to get myself to behave:

- ► *I can't eat the cookies.*
- ► *I have got to stop staying up so late.*
- ► *I need to keep my mouth shut.*

While it's true that God wants us to live self-controlled lives by making moral and healthy choices, I was missing a key point about self-control. Read the list directly before this paragraph again. Underline the first word in each statement, which identifies the person trying to do all the work. Who is it?

Notice that in statements like these—which we tell ourselves all the time—everything depends on you and me. But God has been teaching me that self-control is not about getting myself to do something. Self-control is actually about handing control over to God. Otherwise, self-control is just another thing that my inner control freak will try to manage.

*When you are obedient in the wait,
God will be faithful in the work. And
you will be awed in the wonder.*

YOUR STORY

When you consider the word *self-control*, what thoughts come to mind? How would you define it?

As I mentioned earlier, the Greek word for self-control is *enkráteia*, which means "true mastery from within." On a scale of 1 to 10, how much mastery do you feel you have when it comes to self-control? Are you highly impulsive, highly self-controlled, or somewhere in between?

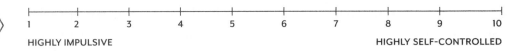

| 1 | 2 | 3 | 4 | 5 | 6 | 7 | 8 | 9 | 10 |

HIGHLY IMPULSIVE   HIGHLY SELF-CONTROLLED

Think about areas of your life where you struggle to maintain self-control. Consider your food, drink, behaviors, and anger. Think about how you use your free time. In what areas do you feel like you need more self-control? You can either write them below or simply take a moment to reflect on them quietly with the Lord.

I am guessing that if you are aware of your weaknesses, you've already tried various methods for negating those unhealthy impulses. If your issue is food, you may have tried certain diet plans. If your issue is anger, you've perhaps taken an anger-management course. There are many self-help books, methods, and techniques by which we can gain mastery over our impulses. How have those methods worked for you? How have they helped you? How have they failed you?

Some of those methods really do work! But the problem with many of them is this: They rely heavily on personal power rather than on acknowledging our powerlessness. The founders of Alcoholics Anonymous must have known the irony of this truth: There is great power in our own powerlessness. Step 1 for people in AA is this: "We admitted we were powerless over our addiction—that our lives had become unmanageable."

How does the idea of powerlessness strike you today, as you consider areas where you lack self-control? How might the admission of your powerlessness be helpful as you begin to live a more self-controlled life?

Take a moment to let the Holy Spirit speak to you about God's power at work inside of you, even as you yourself are powerless. To get God's perspective, read the following verses and record the ways God is speaking to you through each passage.

Proverbs 25:28

Romans 7:15-19

Romans 8:9

Galatians 5:22-23

Read Galatians 2:20. Fill in the blanks.

I have been crucified with Christ and I no longer live, but _____ _____ ___ ___.

This verse isn't simply saying that you ought to live more like Christ. (Of course, you should!) But this verse goes much deeper, saying that Christ actually lives within you!

Where are you feeling powerless and weak today? Know this: He lives within you. His power is made perfect in your weakness (see 2 Corinthians 12:9).

Write a short prayer to God, thanking him for strengthening you where you feel weak today.

THEIR STORY

Let's go straight to Jesus' final hours on earth for a powerful lesson in self-control. Throughout his life, Jesus exhibited perfect self-control and perfect submission to the Father. Turn with me to the Gospel of Luke to see how his self-control was more than a virtue that kept him from doing wrong things. He had so much self-control that it helped him do the right things, the hard things, the unfathomable things, and the painful things.

Read Luke 22:39-43. Write Jesus' words to the Father below.

Imagine the foreknowledge Jesus would have had about the physical suffering to come. That cup also contained God's wrath against every sin, every harsh word, every murder, every adulterous act, every lie, every theft, every injustice that had been or would be committed in all times and in all places by all people, including you and me. Of course Jesus would have preferred not to drink from this cup.

Take a moment to reflect on the cup Jesus was willing to drink from in order to redeem you and restore the perfectly loving relationship he had intended when he created Adam and Eve. As you do so, consider the significance of this moment in the garden of Gethsemane.

If you would like, write a few words to express how you feel when confronted with this knowledge.

Now consider the amount of self-control it took for Jesus to say these words: "Yet not my will, but yours be done."

This is surrender in its most extraordinary form. Some might say that surrender looks like weakly giving up or giving in. But it's very clear that surrender might be the bravest act of all.

You may be thinking, *Well, Jesus was God, so surrender would come easier for him.* But don't forget that Jesus was also fully human. He made himself small before the Father, kneeling down and saying, "Not my will, but yours be done."

Can we make ourselves that small too? As I was studying these Scriptures for this Bible study, I almost missed a critical part of how God intervenes when we need to live as self-controlled, surrendered souls.

Take another look at Luke 22:39-43, focusing especially on verse 43. Jesus did not have to muster up strength on his own. How do we know? Write the verse in the space provided.

Where do you need God's help today? Cry out to Jesus. He knows exactly the way you feel—and then some. Cry out . . . and believe that he will send you an angel today.

Maybe that angel will be the kind you cannot see, a ministering spirit in the spiritual realm. Or maybe that angel is the kind you can see with your own eyes. Maybe that angel is the nurse in your mom's hospital room. Maybe that angel is your sister who showed up to help during a trying time in your family. Maybe that angel is a dear friend who texted you this morning with hope-filled words. I encountered all three of those angels today.

Long ago, God sent reinforcements for his Son before Jesus completed the most sacrificial act in the history of humankind. Don't doubt for a second that he would do the same thing for you.

GETTING YOUR CONTROL UNDER CONTROL

Let's apply the principles we've learned to our own lives. It's not enough to simply try to do the right things. It's not enough to keep a certain set of rules, strive to be better people, or muster up the strength to resist sin. Those approaches make faith about us instead of about Jesus.

Humanity gets this all twisted up. We are bent on trying to find the systems and rules so we can apply them and earn our way. But faith in Jesus doesn't work like that. Christianity is more than a rule book. Christ's power goes where we could never venture on our own.

Where in your life do you need to pray this prayer: "Not my will, but yours be done"? How hard is it to pray that prayer today? If it is difficult, why is that?

Surrender is definitely not for wimps. As I write in *It's All Under Control*, "Don't think about surrendering control as giving up. Think of it as giving in to a greater power" (page 17).

Self-control is actually less about struggling to gain control over your life and more about handing that control to God. It's not about harnessing your personal power but letting God's power strengthen you. If Jesus needed that kind of strength to exhibit self-control, we do too.

I'm not sure where you need reinforcements today. Maybe you struggle with issues of food. Maybe you can't get control over your angry reactions. Maybe you've been wanting to wake up for prayer at six every morning but find your-self hitting the snooze button instead.

Read Luke 22:43 again and record your thoughts as you consider that God sends in reinforcements.

For much of this lesson, we've established that self-control comes from God, not the self. I love this explanation of true self-control: "True self-control is a gift from above, produced in and through us by the Holy Spirit. Until we own that it is received from outside ourselves, rather than whipped up from within, the effort we give to control our own selves will redound to our praise, rather than God's."[5]

On Your Own

Review your response to the question on page 2 of this study: "What do you hope to gain by the end of our journey together?" Do you feel this experience has helped you reach those goals? Are there any new goals you would like to set as you move forward? If so, jot them below.

As you conclude this study, know that you are never really "on your own." Call on Jesus. He'll send reinforcements.

Yet the word *self* is in *self-control* for a reason. Why do you suppose that is?

In her study *Living beyond Yourself,* Beth Moore explains the role of the self in the life of the Christian: "Christ has given us the victory over our flesh, our world, and our accuser. Only self can re-extend authority to one of these three enemies. They cannot presume authority over us. In the life of a believer, they can rule only where they are invited."[6]

I need to know that my own self, powerless as I feel sometimes, can "re-extend" Christ's authority and victory. Of course, that is true only when I submit myself to God's loving rule in my life. I will fail, every time, if I assume I am powerful enough to resist the world and the accuser on my own.

The same goes for you. You can re-extend Christ's control over every temptation, every condition, and every behavior in your life. If you believe God will strengthen you when you ask for that power, then all of these can be true for you:

- ► Food doesn't have control over you.
- ► Alcohol doesn't have control over you.
- ► Anger doesn't have control over you.
- ► Negative thinking doesn't have control over you.
- ► _____ [fill in the blank] doesn't have control over you.

As you learn to live a more self-controlled life, know this: If you belong to Christ, the medal of victory is already yours. Your job is to run the race and claim it.

Read 1 John 4:4 aloud, like a battle cry: "You, dear children, are from God and have overcome them, because the one who is in you is greater than the one who is in the world."

PRAYER

Throughout this study, my prayer has been that we would learn to trust God more than ever before and learn to make our whole lives *about him*. In your own words, write a prayer to God, the one who has it all under control.

You surrender outcomes, but you don't surrender effort. God will call you to do hard things, and with his Spirit pulsing through you, you are more than able.

Epilogue

⋀⋀⋀⋀

YOU DID IT! You persevered to the end. Nobody said this would be easy, but I hope you've decided it was worth it. You worked so hard to get here. If I were with you in real life right now, I'd totally give you a hug, or a fist bump—depending on your personal space issues, of course.

Before you close this study, take a moment to reflect on how you felt at the beginning of this journey. Remember those areas of unhealthy control that you identified? Look how you've grown since then. Good-bye, unhealthy control. Hello, freedom!

You've let go of what God has *not* asked you to do, so you can shine at what he *has*! That's the power of Jesus Christ at work in you.

This isn't the end of the journey, though. This is a new beginning. As you move forward, resist the urge to fall into old patterns of behavior. Refuse to let worry rule your life. Let go of guilt and self-reliance. Hang on to the promises of God.

And lastly, keep those hands open, palms faced up to the sky. God can't put anything into our hands when they are tightened into fists.

Girlfriend, surrender never looked so beautiful.

Jennifer

Leader's Guide

⋀⋀⋀⋀

THANK YOU FOR STEPPING UP to lead this *It's All Under Control Bible Study* in your church or community! Facilitating a group is an important commitment, but I don't want it to feel like a daunting one.

My heart is so tender toward you. Many years ago, I felt God stirring in my spirit, asking me to lead a Bible study in our rural community. I remember thinking, *Who, me?* I didn't feel qualified, but I couldn't deny that I felt called. I put an ad in the newspaper and a few flyers around town. That first night, fifty women showed up. I was so nervous. Thankfully, God reminded me that they didn't show up to hear what I had to say or to eat whatever overbaked cookies I was serving. They came because they were hungry for Jesus. I hope that's an encouragement to you—whether you are a rookie or a veteran leader. I know how much you care for the women who are coming to your study and how deeply you desire to help them grow in faith.

I also know you have many other responsibilities, so I've created this leader's guide to eliminate the guesswork and (I hope) the stress from leading this study.

Prayer: Starting today, commit to praying for the women who will join your study. As they begin to sign up, pray for them by name. Tape a printed list of the names inside the front of your participant guide. Once you begin meeting, pray for each woman every week. Consider enlisting a prayer partner to offer additional prayer support for the spoken and unspoken needs of everyone in your group. As you pray, ask the Holy Spirit to move mightily in your group, to guide you as you lead, and to reveal fresh insights to everyone.

Graphics: Several graphics are available for your use as you spread the word about your forthcoming study. We have prepared graphics for you that are perfectly sized for Instagram, Facebook cover photos, PowerPoint slides, and more. Find them all at www.ItsAllUnderControlBook.com/Resources.

Videos: Short teaching videos that correspond with each week's lesson are available at www.ItsAllUnderControlBook.com/Resources. You may choose to show these at the beginning of each session. This is optional bonus content that is available to you free of charge. Be sure to let the women in your group know if you will be watching the video as a group or if you prefer they watch it at home.

Free printables: Remind the women in your group that they can download and print several images with inspiring quotes and Bible verses to display in their homes or offices. These are available at www.ItsAllUnderControlBook.com/Resources.

First timers: Consider inviting new people to your group, and be aware that some of them may have never attended a Bible study before. A great way to make first timers feel welcome is to give them the workbook as a gift.

Split into groups: If more than a dozen people sign up for your study, consider dividing the large group into smaller groups to facilitate better discussions and allow everyone to share their thoughts. The ideal size for a small group is six to ten people. Ask spiritually mature women in your group to prayerfully consider leading the small groups. Ask those leaders to review this guide before the first session.

Create a comfortable environment: Plan ahead by making sure you have a distraction-free environment. Consider noise, lighting, privacy, cleanliness, and seating. Snacks and drinks are nice, but don't stress yourself out. A pitcher of ice water and some fresh fruit, dark chocolate, or tortilla chips are adequate. If you have an especially large group, consider asking other women to take turns bringing snacks.

Let silence do its work: When facilitating sessions, be prepared for the occasional awkward silence. If you feel like the quiet in your small group has gone on a bit too long, wait just a few seconds longer. People often need time to formulate their responses or gain the courage to speak out loud.

Affirm people: Always try to find a way to encourage those who mustered up the courage to share in a group. Don't simply move on to the next question. You can affirm those who speak up by thanking them or pointing out an insightful remark they made. People are less likely to share if they feel as if you're looking only for the "right answer."

Emphasize confidentiality: There's nothing scarier in a Bible study than sharing a deeply personal story. Remind everyone that confidentiality is expected from all.

Complete the weekly assignments: Let everyone know that they should complete the assigned week's study before you meet. Encourage them to answer all the questions in their workbooks, whether or not they choose to share them out loud with the group.

A framework for your time together

You are free to lead your study at the pace you like. One possible approach: Schedule six sessions of two hours each. If you have a 7 p.m. start time, your evening might look like this:

7 p.m.	Meet, greet, and catch up with one another.
7:10 p.m.	Group prayer.
7:15 p.m.	Watch the video available at www.ItsAllUnderControlBook.com/Resources (optional).
7:30 p.m.	Break into small groups and go through the weekly assignment. As a leader you are encouraged to center your discussion on the questions in the workbook. There probably won't be time to answer all of the questions as a group, so feel free to pick the ones that might stir up the most meaningful discussion. Also, before you move on to the next section or page, consider asking the group, "Was there anything else on this page that you would like to discuss?"
8:30 p.m.	Take prayer requests from members of your small group. Pray specifically for individual requests.
8:50 p.m.	Remind participants to: ▸ complete the next assignment ▸ complete the assigned readings from *It's All Under Control* ▸ continue to hold one another up in prayer through the week
8:55 p.m.	Dismiss your group.

Blessings on you as you begin this journey. God has equipped you for this!

Running Smarter

Let us strip off every weight that slows us down, especially the sin that so easily trips us up. And let us run with endurance the race God has set before us.

HEBREWS 12:1, NLT

Think through your responsibilities—such as work, household duties, family, and friendships. Then consider other "weights," including unhealthy coping mechanisms, toxic relationships, and commitments made only to please others.

In the "My Race" column, list the items that you sense are yours to fulfill. Under "Junk in the Trunk," list the items that God may be calling you to "strip off" because they slow you down and aren't yours to carry. Look over your two lists. Praise God for the beautiful parts, and ask his help for the hard parts. Then seek his help in removing the junk in the trunk, bit by bit.

My Race

Junk in the Trunk

I Am Not the Christ

Ask God to bring to mind times in your life when you've had good motives that ended with bad results. Consider times when you've tried to take over a child's school project, resolve a conflict on someone else's behalf, "fix" your spouse, or create a memorable experience only to have it stress you out (along with everyone else).

Write down a word or phrase that represents those times in your life. Behind each one of them, write, "I am not the Christ." For example:

Without her asking, I told my friend why her boyfriend is wrong for her.　　*I am not the Christ.*

_____　　_____

_____　　_____

_____　　_____

_____　　_____

_____　　_____

_____　　_____

_____　　_____

_____　　_____

_____　　_____

_____　　_____

_____　　_____

_____　　_____

Who Are You?

Cracking the control code will require each of us to take a sober assessment of our identity. What makes you who you are? If you feel stumped as you consider that question, think of it another way by asking yourself this: "What are the things that, if they were taken away, would shatter the identity I have created?" To spark your thinking, consider your work, your family, your relationships, the stuff you own, the way you look, the longings you have.

One by one, commit to turning over control in each of those areas to God.

Begin to make your primary identity this:
"The one whom Jesus keeps on loving."

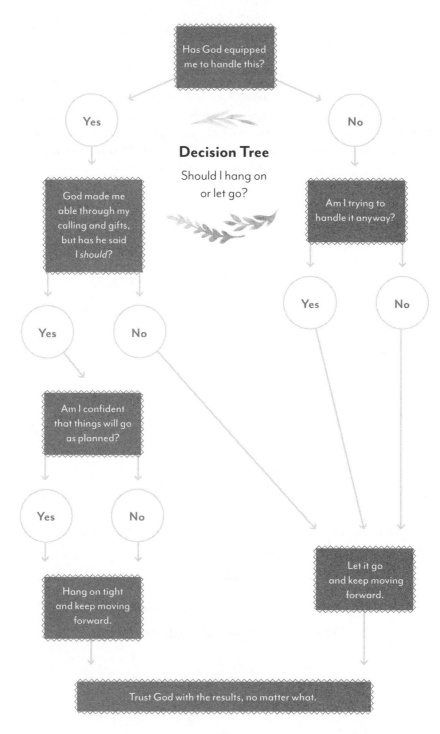

Has God equipped me to handle this?

Yes

No

Decision Tree

Should I hang on or let go?

God made me able through my calling and gifts, but has he said I *should*?

Am I trying to handle it anyway?

Yes

No

Yes

No

Am I confident that things will go as planned?

Yes

No

Hang on tight and keep moving forward.

Let it go and keep moving forward.

Trust God with the results, no matter what.

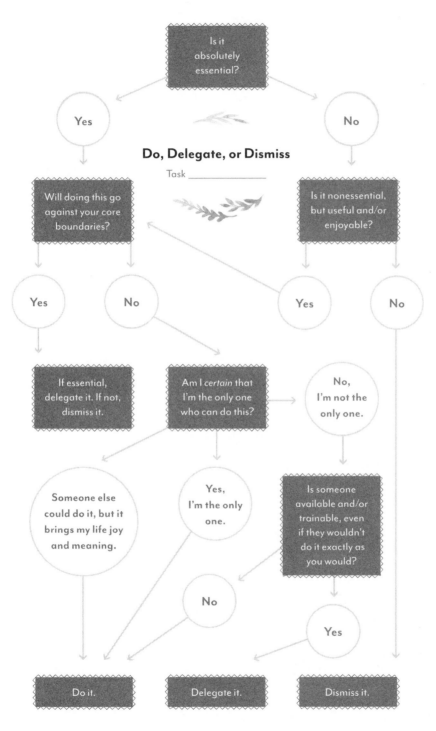

Do, Delegate, or Dismiss

Task _____

Endnotes

1. This prayer is also included in a foreword I wrote for Suzanne Eller's book *The Spirit-Led Heart* (Bloomington, MN: Bethany House, 2018) and is printed here with permission. I highly recommend this resource for anyone seeking to move from a self-led heart to a Spirit-led heart.
2. Charles H. Spurgeon, *Devotional Classics of C. H. Spurgeon*, Jay Green, ed. (Lafayette, IN: Sovereign Grace Publishers, 1990), July 24, Morning.
3. Shelly Miller, *Rhythms of Rest* (Bloomington, MN: Bethany House, 2016), 16–17.
4. *Strong's Concordance*, s.v. "enkráteia."
5. David Mathis, "Self-Control and the Power of Christ," Desiring God, October 8, 2014, https://www.desiringgod.org/articles/self-control-and-the-power-of-christ.
6. Beth Moore, *Living beyond Yourself* (Nashville: LifeWay, 2004), 201.

About the Author

⋀⋀⋀⋀

JENNIFER DUKES LEE is also the author of *The Happiness Dare* and *Love Idol*. She is a popular blogger, writer for DaySpring's (in)courage, and a speaker at women's conferences across the United States. Her words have been featured on numerous podcasts, radio programs, Proverbs 31 Ministries, Fox News *Opinion*, the *Des Moines Register*, and *Today's Christian Woman*.

A former news reporter for several Midwestern newspapers, Jennifer still loves to chase a great story. Nowadays, however, she prefers to write about the remarkably good news of Jesus Christ.

Jennifer is known for her authentic voice, as she encourages women to walk in freedom. She clings to the hope of the Cross and is passionate about sharing the gospel through story. She believes in miracles; she is one. She marvels at God's unrelenting grace for people who mess up—stumbling sinners like her, who have been made whole through Christ.

Jennifer and her husband live on the Lee family farm, where they raise crops, pigs, and two beautiful humans. She attends a small country church where some Sundays you'll find her spinning tunes as the church DJ. She's a big fan of dark chocolate, emojis, eighties music, bright lipstick, and Netflix binges. She wants to live life in such a way that you can't help but want more of Jesus.

Visit Jennifer online at www.JenniferDukesLee.com. She invites you to join her on Twitter and Instagram, @dukeslee, and on Facebook at www.facebook.com/JenniferDukesLee.

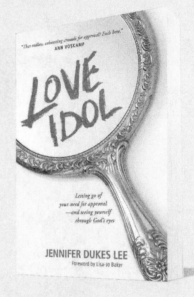